The Urban Gardening Guide

How To Create A Thriving Garden In An Apartment, On A Patio, Balcony, Rooftop Or Other Small Spaces

James Gipson

This book is dedicated to everyone living in small or limited spaces. Your garden is only limited by your imagination.

Copyright Act of 1976, the scanning, uploading and electronic sharing of any part of this book without the explicit written consent or permission of the publisher constitutes unlawful piracy and the theft of intellectual property.

If you would like to use material or content from this book (other than for review purposes), prior written permission must be obtained from the publisher.

You can contact the publishing company at admin@speedypublishing.com. Thank you for not infringing on the author's rights.

Speedy Publishing LLC (c) 2014
40 E. Main St., #1156
Newark, DE 19711
www.speedypublishing.co

Ordering Information:
Quantity sales; Special discounts are available on quantity purchases by corporations, associations, and others. For details, contact the "Special Sales Department" at the address above.

This is a reprint book.

Manufactured in the United States of America

Table of Contents

Publisher's Notes i

Chapter 1: About Urban Gardening 1

Chapter 2: Gardening In Apartments 3

Chapter 3: Trees That Thrive Indoors 10

Chapter 4: Can You Grow Fruits And Vegetables Indoors? 14

Chapter 5: Hydroponic Gardening Indoors 18

Chapter 6: Caring For Inside Plants 21

Chapter 7: How To Winterize A Balcony Garden 26

Chapter 8: Fertilizing Tips 29

Chapter 9: Pruning Basics 34

Chapter 10: Watering Basics for Indoor Plants 40

Chapter 11: Indoor Plants Need Light 47

Chapter 12: Conclusion 52

Meet the Author 53

More Books by James Gipson 55

Publisher's Notes

Disclaimer

This publication is intended to provide helpful and informative material. It is not intended to diagnose, treat, cure, or prevent any health problem or condition, nor is intended to replace the advice of a physician. No action should be taken solely on the contents of this book. Always consult your physician or qualified health-care professional on any matters regarding your health and before adopting any suggestions in this book or drawing inferences from it.

The author and publisher specifically disclaim all responsibility for any liability, loss or risk, personal or otherwise, which is incurred as a consequence, directly or indirectly, from the use or application of any contents of this book.

Any and all product names referenced within this book are the trademarks of their respective owners. None of these owners have sponsored, authorized, endorsed, or approved this book.

Always read all information provided by the manufacturers' product labels before using their products. The author and publisher are not responsible for claims made by manufacturers.

Chapter 1: About Urban Gardening

When one thinks of gardens and gardening we don't think of city life. We think of grass, trees and nature. Gardens bring to mind the beauty of the country side. But, there are those people today that want to have a touch of nature in their homes even though they live in a metropolis like New York.

Urban Gardening is a way of overcoming the restrictions that the city brings with its lack of nature. This is due primarily to the fact that the natural landscape becomes destroyed because of the buildings and concrete. By creating gardens within limited city spaces such as in apartments one can have a touch of nature close to them.

Just because one lives in a concrete city doesn't mean one doesn't seek a way to have green in their lives. Today there are many creative ways to incorporate gardens living in a city environment. You can look up and see window boxes hanging from windows with flowers and plants. People do container gardening in their homes. Now days both people and their communities utilize spaces like roofs tops as well as empty lots to create urban gardens. Those with terraces attached to their apartments can add a little garden right out their doors. Urban gardening is a way to reconnect with nature in a man-made environment.

Urban gardening and agriculture is becoming increasingly more important as many contractors are buying fertile land and building on it. This means that less and less space is becoming available to grow things as a result. The farmers who grow fruits and vegetables are being slowly closed out of land to grow on. Therefore urban gardening is a resourceful way to grow plants and vegetables in the city. It is without a doubt that as more and more cities spring up urban fruit and vegetable gardens are quickly becoming another source for food worldwide. It has been shown through recent studies that aside from the ascetic beauty that urban gardens bring to city areas; urban vegetable gardens have been able to serve as food source in the poorer urban neighborhoods. For many of the world wide impoverished areas this is their only source of fresh fruits and vegetables. Urban gardens are being viewed more than just a way to beautify a city landscape. They are considered sources to improve the environment, community builders and a possible food source for families.

Gardens in an urban environment can vary according to its location, size and the climate depending on where it's placed. Depending where it is located, it is possible to have a garden grow year round in a city. A balcony is an ideal possibility for such a garden. It is also feasible to have a year round indoor garden in an apartment. All it takes is a little know how and a lot of creativity.

Chapter 2: Gardening In Apartments

In the cramped city where there is not too much room people still want to have nature around them. People are finding ways to create a little space in their apartments and homes to grow what they want indoors. All you need in order to have an indoor garden are three things; light, soil and water. It doesn't have to be the kind of soil in a back yard either. In local plant stores there are growing mediums and soils that are available. There are premixed growing mediums that have things like nutrients in them to grow plants quite efficiently.

The first consideration in your apartment for an urban garden is that you need to find the right location in your home. If you have a balcony or patio that will work too. You need to take into consideration the environmental conditions of either the room or balcony space you choose. Things like lighting and temperature help you pick a space that will enable a plant to grow. These factors will also help you decide which plants are the best choices for your space. For example, if you like plants in each room you may even want plants in your bathroom. In this case you have to take into consideration that it is generally the most humid room in the house without much light. So with this in mind you would need a plant that does well in low light and humidity. These are the conditions in most bathrooms.

Regardless of the location you choose in your home for your indoor garden; it should have a minimum 6 to 8 hours of sunlight each day. If you don't have a lot of sunlight daily you can purchase plant lights to give your plants the light they need to flourish. Interesting enough it is suggested that you do not put a plant directly on the window sill. This is because the window sill reflects and magnifies the sun rays and can overwhelm a plant. Some people who may not have the space or conditions in their homes may even get permission from their buildings to use the roof to make a garden on.

Today many people are making gardens in containers that thrive. Small spaces and container planting seems to go hand in hand. When you do container planting you can use conventional plant pots which come in different sizes and materials at the local plant store. Or if you rather, you can make your own containers from things like a milk carton to plant in. The main thing is that a plant pot or any other container you use must have at least a hole on the bottom for drainage. This allows for excess water to run out of the hole when you water the plant.

The main requirement for maintaining your indoor garden is consistency. Plants thrive in a stable environment. The more you do to regulate the maintenance of your garden or plants the better they will do. This means you need to water your garden or plants regularly. Watering of course based on how much a specific plant needs. You also need to have a regulated feeding schedule for the plants as well as having the correct light and consistent temperature. You have to periodically remove the dead leaves and wipe the dust that may accumulate gently from the leaves to keep your plants healthy. Spraying them in between watering is also good if they appear dry.

TRIED & TRUE PLANTS THAT DO WELL INDOORS:

Low Maintenance Plants (Do well when watered once a month)

Pothos (Epipremnum aureum (syn.Pothos aureus, Raphidophora aureum, or Scindapsus aureus) - This plant survives from being in places like offices to college dorm rooms. It has heart shaped green leaves with yellow and white variegation. The leaves trail on clumping vine. (Hanging type Plant). This plant is very tough. It requires low light and needs water once a month. The worst plant person can keep this one alive.

Spider Plant (Chlorophytum bischetii, or more usually C. comosum (syn.C. capense) - This plant likes medium light and has excellent air and filtering qualities that are approved by NASA. It is a grasslike, clump forming evergreen perennial in the lily Family. As it grows small white flowers form with seed capsules (these are baby spider plants) They do not do well in frost.

Snake Plants (Mother in Laws Tongue) Sansevaria trifasciata (syn. S.zeylandica) - These plants are also tough. They require just a little more light than in a closet and not too much water. Many times these plants suffer from overwatering. This is a low light plant. Too much sun may bleach them causing them to lose their color. There are over thirty varieties of snake plants available. It gets its name because of the shape of its leaves and the name **"Mother in Laws Tongue"** because of the sharpness of the leaves.

Bromelaids - Bromelaids is a family of Manocot Flowering plants of around 2,400 species: including pineapples. Many of these flowering plants have the ability to store water in their overlapping bases that form a tank. There are some the produce flowers as well. Bromeliads are perennial monocotyledons - plants that have one seed leaf like lilies or corn. Of course you want the type that does well indoors. You can go to ask your local plant store to ask which will do best in the environment you have at home.

Moderate Care Plants (Require watering more than once a month)

Dragon Trees (Dracaena draco, D. fragrans, D. marginata or D. sanderiana) - Dragon trees are a species of about 40 trees and shrubs. The most popular one found indoors is the **Madagascar Dragon Tree**. This group of plants seems to be low to moderate light and drought tolerant; but the soil should be kept moist. If the leaves start to brown it means you need more humidity in the atmosphere. Long narrow spike like leaves characterize the foliage. The foliage is usually green with a red outline.

Sword Fern (Nephrolepsis cordifolia, N. exaltata [the cultivar 'Bostoniensis' - Sword Fern is the famous Boston Fern (obliterata) This variety of fern tolerates variant light levels. It is tolerant of drier conditions compared to other ferns. Sword Fern is a large ever green plant with straight leaves. The leaves are straight to curving blades with sharp tooth alternate leaflets. The leaves form from thick, woody scaly rhizome.

Jade Plants (Crassula ovata syn. C.argentea or C. portulaca. Occasionally species C. arborescens or C. falcata are found for sale). You need fairly strong light for this plant even though it's indoors. Because of the coin shaped jade green leaves it is considered by the Chinese a Feng Shui plant. One down side of keeping this plant is its susceptibility to mealy bugs when it is in a declining state. Mealy bugs can be treated with a Q-tip and alcohol to wipe them away. Moderate water and good light will help keep this plant in optimum shape.

Plants That Need a Little Loving (These plants need attention)

Bonsai (Various spp.) - These are various species of miniature trees that were originally made famous because of the Japanese Art of Bonsai. They are now found throughout Asia, primarily China (known as Penjing), Thailand, Vietnam and other cultures as well. Bonsai require a lot of care. When you get a Bonsai plant; the plant store or person you buy them from can tell you the best way to maintain them based on your home's environment.

Orchids (Family *Orchidaceae*) - Are a diverse family of flowers and plants. They are virtually found on every continent except Antarctica. All orchids require higher humidity than most other plants in the home.

Recommendation orchid for the beginner is: **Cattleya spp w**hich is brought indoors in Florida and in the North in the Winters. These orchids need 60 degrees at night and 70 during the day. 50-60% humidity is necessary to keep these orchids thriving as well as good indirect sunlight.

African Violets *(Saintpaulia ionantha)* - There are literally hundreds of cultivars and species now of African Violets. Bottom watering is key for this plant. The two biggest enemies to this plant are crown rot and leaf spotting due to watering incorrectly. Water has to be kept away from the crown and leaves so it can thrive. African Violets also require higher humidity like orchids and good indirect light.

So these are just a few of the plants you can grow in your home not to mention vegetables and herbs too. On the plus side with indoor gardening you can grow things regardless of the weather conditions outside. If you have a tall roof with narrow spacing; shade tolerant plants such as South African native ***Afrocarpus falcate*** commonly known as **Sickle-leaved Yellowwood** and **False Yellowwood** or **Outeniqua Yellowwood;** can do well.

If you have shelf space only in your home try succulents and cactuses. Bulb plants and flowers make excellent indoor plant choices as well. You have to however utilize the conditions in your home to force them to bloom at times like January indoors. The trick is to simulate the habitat (in this case one's home) of the plant naturally at the time you want it to bloom. This way you can have yearlong flowers indoors.

Watering

Now a word on watering. Plants suffer from over watering as much as from being under watered. So, it makes one wonder how much is enough for a plant to thrive. First of all it depends on the type of plant it is. Different plants require different amounts of water to survive and grow. When you purchase them you must get watering instructions. Make sure to ask the local plant store if you are not sure about how to water your plant.

Along with the type of plant you have other considerations also determine the amount of water you need for your plants. Things like your home environment's humidity and light levels also have to be considered as well as the pot the plants are in when watering your plant. For example, a terra cotta pot absorbs more water than a plastic container. So, you may have to water a plant more if you home is dry and you are using terra cotta pots. All these things affect the amount of water a plant requires. Although not as attractive; plastic pots help retain the soils moisture better than ceramic or terra cotta pots.

In colder climates the air tends to be drier. Because of this factor you may have to purchase an humidifier or increase watering depending on the type of plant you have. Higher need plants like bonsai and orchids do well with a humidity tray. To make a humidity tray all you need is a tray that is filled with pebbles and water almost covering the pebbles. The plant is placed on the pebbles and not directly in the water. As the water evaporates it creates humidity for the plant.

After a while you start to develop a sense of how much or how little to water your indoor garden. If you are a beginner and are not sure about how much water or moisture to give your plants they do have moister meters available. They stick into the soil as a gauge to let you know if you need to water your plants or not.

Feeding

Fertilizers and plant food are very important for indoor gardens. There are general varieties as well as some that are for specific plants. The general ones are easier to use than the plant specific ones. You have to pay attention to proportions though. Too much feeding can harm the plants. There are fertilizing sticks that can be placed in the soil monthly to feed the plants. This may be the easiest for you. You can ask your local plant store to give you the correct fertilizer for your plants with the proper instructions. Some soils and growing mediums have the plant food or fertilizer already included in their mixture.

Repotting

Most plants have to be repotted because they grow. Plants do outgrow the containers and pots they are in from time to time. You can tell when this happens because the roots will start to grow out through the drainage holes or coil around the containers inner edges.

So, the first thing you do is of course is to get a bigger container or pot for the plant. Make sure there is a drain hole or holes at the bottom. You want to layer the bottom of the pot or container with either rocks, shards of pottery or wood chips. These help with the drainage and prevent the soil from coming through the holes.

Next, fill the container with soil up to where you want the roots to rest. Gently loosen the roots of the plant from the old pot and lift it to the new one. Rest it on the soil in the new pot and fill the area around it with remaining soil. Fill it up to approximately one inch from the top of the container. Once the plant is snug in the new pot, soak the soil so it is good and wet.

If a plant is so large it has to remain in the pot it's in; then you can loosen the top three inches of the soil that is in that pot and remove it. Replace the removed soil with fresh soil and/or humus. This is known as top dressing. Top dressing is a method that is used because the plant is too big to be repotted. You use this method because you can see the root ball when you scrape off the upper soil layers. That lets you know how big the plant is. Removing the three inches from the top soil lets you know where the plants limit is in the pot. The same thing occurs in nature in the ground. This technique should be done on a yearly basis. A plant can last decades this way. Replacing soil this way is also done as a foundation in Bonsai.

These are just the basics on how to start and maintain a garden in your apartment. As you learn about each plant you have you will know what they need. Each plant is different and each needs to be cared for in a specific way.

Chapter 3: Trees That Thrive Indoors

Interesting enough there are some tropical trees that do well indoors. These trees bear fruit and can actually grow in one's home. With a little care and indoor pollination know how you can grow these plants indoors.

Indoor Pollination

Outdoors plants have natural pollinators. In apartments this is not possible unless you have a balcony or patio. Indoors we have to help plants that need pollination. All you need to do is take a camel hair paintbrush to transfer pollen from the antlers of the plants flower or fruit antlers to the plants stigmatic surface. It doesn't have to be exact. Jiggle the floral parts of the plant with the brush and that is all it takes for the plant to pollinate. The plants described below are what are called "perfect flowers". This means they have both the male and female parts and self-fertilize. With this method of jiggling the antlers it gives them an extra boost.

Tropical Trees You Can Grow Indoors

Here is a list of tropical trees you can grow indoors. Like I stated above they produce perfect flowers which makes it easier for them to be grown indoors because of self-pollination properties.

Carissa macrocarpa (Natal Plum)

This is a familiar house plant and also an indoor bonsai. This plant is native to South Africa. Natal Plum plants need sunlight and are drought resistant although you don't want the soil to dry out. Its good if this plant can be taken outside in the Summer (If you have a summer house or a balcony). It has a vigorous woody shrub. If given the right space and conditions it grows to 18 feet tall!!! The foliage is evergreen and produces long 2 inch white flowers. The fruit it bears the actual "Natal Plum" can grow up to 2 inches long and 1/14 inches wide. As the plums ripen they turn a bright magenta red. When fully ripe the fruit is protein rich. It can be eaten off the tree or made into jellies, syrups, gelatin based desserts, pies and tarts.

The Natal Plum Tree should be fertilized regularly with all-purpose plant food. The cuttings are very difficult to root. It's best to use seeds to grow this plant.

Eugenia uniflora (Surinam Cherry)

Although it is indigenous to Surinam and Guiana this plant is found throughout the Caribbean. You can find the Surinam Cherry as a shrub throughout Florida. If given the chance it grows to 25 feet and produces aromatic foliage. Its flowers look like powder puffs. They are white and long stalked. The fruit which grows is from ½ inch to 1 1/2 inch wide and changes from green to bright red to dark plum color. Its flesh is both tart and sweet and an excellent source of Vitamin A. It contains one large and three small seeds, which are resinous and should not be eaten. The fruit ripens quickly within 3 weeks after flowering. The fruit can be eaten as is or chilled and or sprinkled with sugar. This shrub needs lots of sun light. It is not however fussy about the soil. Let the soil dry out in between watering. Fertilize it regularly with its active growth; flowering and fruiting usually occur late in the summer.

Malpighia emarginata (Barbados Cherry)

This tree is native to the Lesser Antilles from St. Croix to Trinidad. It is a small tree that can grow up to 20 feet tall. Its foliage is waxy, oblong and dark green. It has delicate flowers that grow in twos and threes along the stem, each containing either lavender or pink spoon shaped fringed petals. The plant produces three lobed one inch tangy bright red cherries. Very high in Vitamin C they are second only to Rose Hips of the Rosa Rugosa plant. Depending on a person's preference the seeds can be eaten. It's best to give this plant a southern or southwestern exposure away from drafts. You need a fertile well drained pot with a potting mixture of a pH of 5.5 to 6.5. The soil should be dried out slightly between watering. Do not let the plant sit in a dish that catches the excess water as it drains. Also use an acidifying fertilizer during growth and flowering periods from later in the winter months through late summer. Propagation (growing new plants) can be done from usually half ripe tip cuttings of the plant.

Myrcia floribunda (Rumberry, Guavaberry)

This plant is native to the Caribbean and Southern Mexico. The Rumberry tree is very attractive shrub/tree. Indoors, it can grow to 6 feet as opposed to outdoors and 50 feet. The bark is reddish brown when it matures and the foliage is glossy and dark green. The flowers look like powder puffs in small white clusters. The fruit grows dark red to almost black in color and half an inch in diameter. Rumberry fruit is similar to elderberries with a bitter taste. It can be enjoyed as is or in preserves. In the islands they make different alcoholic drinks with it. This plant likes a lot of sunlight with soil that retains moisture but not soggy. A terra cotta pot is good for this type of plant. Avoid winter drafts with this plant, it is very sensitive to cold.

Pereskia aculeata (Barbados Gooseberry)

This fruit is indigenous to the Caribbean, Northern Coast of South America and Panama. The Barbados Goosberry plant is primarily a shrub that becomes a loosely climbing vine with age. The stems are fleshy and the foliage is elliptical semi deciduous dark green leaves.

The flowers are lemon scented and a creamy white color which appear in the fall. The fruit is pear shaped or oval one to two inches wide upon pollination. Its color ranges from yellow to red. When fully ripe the fruit is juicy and tart but tasty. The soft brown seeds can be eaten. You can eat the fruit when ripe or stew it. It is high in Vitamin A and Calcium. The leaves and stems are cooked and can be eaten as greens. This plant requires full sun light. The soil can be composted enhanced but needs to be very well drained. It is good to use a terra cotta pot for this plant with sand on the bottom for additional drainage. The Gooseberry plant is very sensitive to over watering. It's good to feed it during active growth with water soluble fertilizer. Propagation is easy from seeds or half ripened stem cuttings.

Punica granatum var. *nana* (Dwarf Pomegranate)

This little tree which is originally native to India and Northern Iran has been around since ancient times. It has been cultivated throughout the Mediterranean regions of Asia, Africa and Europe. The straight species can grow from 20 to 30 feet tall. This variety grows to three feet. The Dwarf Pomegranate can bloom at one foot however. It makes a great container plant and is used often as a Bonsai Tree. In normal conditions the leaves are ever green, lance shaped and leathery in texture. At the end of new growths red, white or pinkish flowers appear. The fruit of the Dwarf Pomegranate are round, 2 inches wide and red when ripe. The hard seeds are surrounded by little sacs of pulp which are tart and tasty. You can eat the sacs or juice them. The juice is a natural colorant for cream cheese and frosting. It is also used as a mixer for sparkling water and cocktails. The fruit is high in potassium as well as a fair amount of vitamin C and phosphorus. This plant is easy to grow indoors. It needs a semi dry environment, but keep it away from heaters and radiators. It does well in a good potting soil amended with lime and a good terra cotta pot. Let the soil dry between watering. Do not sit the container in a saucer and let the water drain off. Fertilize it regularly during the spring and summer. These plants are easily propagated from seeds and wood cuttings.

CHAPTER 4: CAN YOU GROW FRUITS AND VEGETABLES INDOORS?

It is indeed possible to grow vegetables and fruit in an apartment. It takes a little research and a little know how to get started. Here are some basics to help in that regard.

The first consideration is to make sure you pick a space in your apartment that has ample sunlight. In some apartments the sun shifts with the seasons so you may find your garden changing rooms seasonally.

Before you actually start on you indoor garden you need to learn as much as you can about the vegetable or fruit plant you want to grow. You have to know what conditions are required for you to produce a successful plant indoors. Most plants grow in different stages and each one of the stages requires a different step to ensure its growth.

When deciding on the type of container you are going to use to grow your fruit or vegetable you have to take into account the size and needs of the plant. You can use any kind of container almost as long as there is at least an ample hole on the bottom for drainage.

For example, is the vegetable or fruit plant you are interested in growing require a lot of watering? Some of the more popular containers used in apartment gardens can be but are not limited to small waste baskets, dish basins, fish tanks, the bottom half of plastic bottles, urns and hanging baskets. Other, more common containers are plastic pots, ceramic containers, window boxes, terra cotta pots and dishes. Terra cotta is very porous and you have to be aware of over drying. Also if you are using wooden boxes you have to be careful with the box rotting from water. To help prevent wooden boxes from rotting it can be lined with plastic or plastic containers can go inside it. On the market today are even several self-watering containers. They range from $12.99 to $39.99 depending on size and quality. They are good for those who are not so good with watering routines as well as those who like terra cotta. This way the hydration levels are maintained for the plant and soil. It is also not recommended to use narrow topped containers because they are not good when it comes time to transplant the plant. It's also not good to use gardening soil for indoor or container gardening. It is better to use a good potting soil or a soilless potting mix.

The container you use for your plant has to be in proportion to the side of the plant. If it is not in proportion to the plant size it will affect its growth negatively. As plants grow you transplant them to the next matching size. Also because your plants are not growing in the ground it is important to fertilize them more often. A good method is to use liquid fertilizer and add it to the water every other watering. It's also good to practice indoor pollination because there are no bees indoors. (indoor pollination is explained in chapter 3)

It is suggested that a lighter container is used in warmer weather and that the plant is put in the sun for at least five hours a day. If you don't have ample light you can use artificial plant lights which I will touch upon a little later.

The amount of sunlight you get naturally in your apartment determines the type of plants that are suitable to grow there. All plants need optimum light conditions for photosynthesis to occur. For those who do not get ample sun light there are plants like mushrooms to consider. The rules of thumbs to follow are root and leaf crops (yes your container is your crop) can tolerate partial shade. Vegetables that are grown for their fruit need a minimum of 5 hours direct sunlight daily and at best 8 to 10. The available light can be maximized by using reflective material around the plants like aluminum foil and white surfaces.

Plants need the blue and red light which are both found in sunlight. If your plant only gets a little natural light you can use a wide spectrum florescent light bulb to help supplement the lack of natural light. If your plant gets no sunlight then a full spectrum florescent light bulb is needed for your plant to grow.

When you arrange your plants underneath the florescent light; the bulb has to be within a few inches of the plant. This is to ensure that the plant receives adequate light. The light should be adjusted so it is no more than 6 inches away. This applies to the standard T-12 florescent light bulbs. T-8s or T-5s are much higher in intensity and need to be at least a foot away from the leaves. You can add a strip of aluminum foil to the bottom of the lamp so more light is reflected. Plants also need night time. So it is important to turn off the light after about 12 -16 hours. An automatic timer works good.

Herbs are the easiest food to grow indoors. Next is the small fruited variety of vegetables such as small tomatoes like Tiny Tim or Roma.

Radishes grow very quickly. You take the seeds and scatter them on moist soil in a 6 inch pot. Cover with a ¼ soil and then cover the top with a piece of glass or plastic until the seeds germinate to keep the moisture in. This technique is like a miniature green house. Carrots grow slower but can be grown the same as radishes. Use the small rooted carrots like Little Fingers for best results indoors.

Another way to make a miniature green house is to cut a soda bottle at the base so you have a shorter pot bottom. Make sure you put a whole for drainage in the bottom. Fill the bottom with soil and then insert the seeds in the soil. Use the long top part of the bottle to cover over the bottom. This acts as a green house for your seeds to geminate in. Stick one seed in each section and then place in a dark cupboard until the seeds begin to germinate. You can also germinate your seeds in old egg cartons filled with soil and a seed or two in each section.

The best vegetables to grow indoors are the ones that don't require or take up a lot of space such as carrots, radishes and lettuce; likewise those that fruit over a period of time like tomatoes and peppers. These varieties take up the least amount of space and containers to grow.

You can do things like mix up the planting variety like different lettuces such as arugula and nasturtiums. If picked young spinach and beets work in salads too.

If you are growing vegetables like tomatoes, cucumbers and carrots you can use containers that are large like 15 quart capacity and work your way up if you have the room. Just leave room at the top of the containers for mulching in between. If you are not sure about how many seeds should be planted in a container then look at the back of the seed package or popular gardening guide for plant to pot ratios.

Dwarf and miniature varieties of vegetables and fruits often mature and bear fruit but not as well as the standard varieties.

CHAPTER 5: HYDROPONIC GARDENING INDOORS

Another alternative for growing fruits and vegetables as well as other plants in an apartment is Hydroponic Gardening. Hydroponic gardening allows for growing plants without the use of soil. Instead a nutritive solution is used. It is said with hydroponic gardens many of the headaches with a soil garden is eliminated. This is especially true because no soil means no soil mess, no pests in the soil and less expense. Plants grow in a nutrient rich liquid, eliminating the need for heavy and cumbersome planters and soil.

To have a hydroponic garden all you need is a little space, light and attention to give to the plants. It can be done in space as small as a windowsill or if space allows a larger set up. If space is one of your concerns then hydroponics allows closer placement of plants because extensive root systems are not necessary with the plant cultures. Also with hydroponics the water is recirculated as opposed to watering on a schedule. Another plus is there are virtually no weeds in this kind of garden.

There are two basic types of hydroponic garden systems to consider are water based or media based. The medium is not soil but rather can include composited bark, gravel, peat moss, perlite or vermiculite. Also you have to consider whether you want an active system which requires electric timers and pumps which make it function at optimum level. Or on the other hand there is the passive system which uses a wicking agent to give the plant roots nutrients.

Because the plants are growing in water, their nutrients don't come from soil as with conventional gardens. Nutrient solutions are basically varying types of fertilizers that are added to the water. The idea is that by alternating between giving air flow and nutrient solution to you plants roots the need for soil is by passed. This also enables the possibility of growing plants all year long regardless of outdoor climate factors because it is set up indoors.

The plants receive their nutrients thru a nutrient solution that is applied to the roots via distilled water. The three big nutrients s plant needs are nitrogen, phosphorus and potassium. In addition there are other nutrients called macro nutrients and micro nutrients that the plants need as well which are also incorporated into the nutritive solution. You can either ask your local plant shop or research yourself online or the library to decide which type of set up is best for you. This goes for choosing the best nutritive solution for your planting needs also. You also need to make sure that you pH balance the solution that you feed your plants with.

Here are some basic hydroponic garden setups to consider:

The Ebb and Flow System

The growing plants are suspended in a tray above a shallow container which allow the roots to hang to the floor of the container beneath them. Beneath the container is a reservoir that contains the solution of your choice. A submersible pump (sold where aquariums are sold) pumps the nutrient solution to the roots via the tray. You also have an overflow pipe in the tray so the tray doesn't flow over. Instead the solution is drained back into the reservoir. This gives the roots a chance to get some oxygen which they also require. After the moment of oxygen the pump starts again and the cycle is repeated.

The Nutrient Film Technique

This hydroponic system is similar to the ebb and flow system except for one main difference. Instead of the overflow drain that drains the solution back into the tray beneath as a reservoir, the solution is pumped to a series of angled trays. From there the solution runs down a slope across the roots of the plants and back down into the reservoir. This creates a constant stream motion which allows oxygen to hit the roots as well as keeps the solution mixed and pH balanced.

Continuous Drip System

Depending on your preference you can have an active recovery or not active recovery system. Either way the submersed pump pushes the solution through a pipe that is suspended over the plant roots. Holes in the piping allow for control of the drip size you wish to employ to fall on each plant. If the system is active recovery then the pipe leads back to the reservoir which is located beneath the plants to catch the drips. As a non-recovery system the solution that is utilized gets pumped to potted plants.

As you can see from my brief descriptions of the systems that in hydroponics the plants receive its food from water born suspension. In conventional gardens the plant receives nutrition from dissolved soil born minerals. One of the biggest benefits of hydroponic gardens is you don't use pesticides and there are no pests that always can plague soil grown plants. You can also grow plants in soilless places with hydroponics. You can go to your local plant store and ask for the best starter hydroponic equipment to meet your needs.

CHAPTER 6: CARING FOR INSIDE PLANTS

In addition to adding outdoor beauty indoors in one's home, plants also help keep the indoor environment clean believe it or not. Plants help rid the air of toxins. They assist in oxygen/carbon dioxide exchange. The other benefit of having plants is that it's also easier to care for and clean up after a plant in comparison to a pet. The main choice for the type of house plant you pick if you have small children or pets is if it's poisonous or not. Just like you would keep poisons in a safe place so your little ones don't get into them the same would go for poisonous plants. It is better to get non-poisonous plants when you have small children and pets to consider.

Now let's go over the general steps needed to care for plants indoors. Just because a plant is low maintenance does not mean you can totally do nothing for it at all. All plants require some form of attention. Remember all plants need the following to thrive:

- Sufficient water and humidity
- Reasonable temperatures
- Occasional feeding and grooming
- Adequate light

Most plants come with instruction tags that tell you how to care for them. Here are the basics for taking care of plants in general:

Watering

All plants have a specific way to water them. If there is no instruction tag on the plant or stuck in the soil ask the person in the plant store to give you watering instructions. Even if watering is irregular, plants still need it. When you do water the plant do so thoroughly. Using room temperature water, saturate the plant until water comes through the drain hole or holes at the bottom of the plant container or pot. Some plants have to be watered daily and some once in a while depending on the type of plant it is.

Humidity

Many of the indoor plants we purchase in the local plant store or nursery actually have tropical origins. They are raised in green houses where the air is moist or humid. Compared to their places of origin our homes are like deserts to the plant. Although they adapt to your homes plants do better when the air has moisture in it. It's good to place high humidity plants in the kitchen or bathroom from time to time. This is because these types of plants thrive in humidity and humidity is higher in those rooms. Also grouping plants together is a way for them to grab a little moisture from the air.

Another way to create humid conditions for the plant is to take a saucer put a layer of marbles at the bottom and partially fill it with water. Place the container on top of the marbles. Do not let it sit in the water directly. The idea is for the pot to capture evaporating moisture not to let the it wick (systems to draw nutrient to a *plant*'s *roots* through capillary action) into the root system. That can cause the roots to rot.

Temperature

Plants have comfort levels just like people. They have minimum temperatures that they will tolerate as well as maximum. As rule of thumb the best temperatures for plants indoors are between 65 degrees F and 75 degrees F in the day and 10 degrees cooler at night. You have to be careful with air conditioners and heaters they can wreck havoc on house plants. Plants should not have direct contact with either. It's not recommended that they are placed by ventilation outlets or air shafts either. Use blinds and or Curtains to regulate direct light on plants because some plants are light sensitive as well and can overheat or dry out.

Fertilizing

For house plants it's suggested to use a diluted house plant fertilizer. Remember a little goes a long way. A plant should get enough light and water to feed its self.

Grooming

Grooming plants serves two purposes: one is to keep the leaves clean and the other is to check for pests and diseases. Keeping the leaves wiped if they are dusty helps them to breathe.

Light

The amount of light that your home has naturally in the way of sunlight will help determine what type of plants are best suited for your home. If your home does not get enough natural light then there are artificial plant light alternatives you can purchase. Depending on the way a window faces determines the amount of light it lets in. Remember that curtains and blinds deter light and that flowering plants need more light than green leaf plants.

Low Light Plants: These are plants that survive in minimum light. North facing windows are good for these plants. They also do well in interior locations in a home like on a coffee table or hanging.

Medium/Indirect Light Plants: For these plants the rule is bright light but no direct sun on them. West or South facing windows do these plants well. They can be placed a foot away from the window.

Bright/Direct Light Plants: Need light, light and more light. Put them right on or as close to the window sill as possible facing west or south.

Here is a chart for you to get some ideas about plants and their needs and what makes them favorable to have in a home.

Plant	Light Requirements	Good Features
Cast Iron Plant/Aspidistra elatior	Low	Cold Tolerant
Chinese Evergreen/Aglaonema	Low	Tolerates Dry Air
Dracaena	Low	Many Varieties to choose from
Kentia Palm/Howea forsteriana	Low	Unlike most Palms it tolerates dry, heated air
Philodendron	Low	Vining habits work in hanging baskets as well as containers
Snake Plant/Sansevieria	Low	Insect Resistant
African Violet/Saintpaulia	Medium Indirect	Great combination of foliage and almost constant blooms, likes humidity
Dumb Cane/Dieffenbachia	Medium Indirect	Several Varieties to choose from
Ficus	Medium Indirect	Seldom needs repotting Many varieties of shapes and sizes
Fishtail Palm/Caryota mitis	Medium Indirect	Tolerates lower light better than most Palms

Plant	Light	Notes
Lady Palm/Rhapis excelsa	Medium Indirect	Can tolerate cooler indoor temperatures
Peperomia	Medium Indirect	Semi-Succulent leaves Can tolerate lack of water
Pothos/Epipremnum aureum	Medium Indirect	Vining Habit Tolerates irregular watering
Rubber Plant/Ficus elastica	Medium Indirect	Seldom needs repotting Variety of forms
Schefflera/Brassaia	Medium Indirect	Glossy leaves Likes high humidity
Spider Plant/Chlorophytum comosum	Medium Indirect	Good hanging basket plant. Produces stems that can be potted and produce new plants
Aloe/Aloe barbadensis	Bright Direct	Freshly succulent leaves that have a nice texture
Cactus(Various)	Bright Direct	Very easy to care for There are many attractive varieties that are sturdy
Croton/Codiaeum	Bright Direct	Variety of Foliage colors available
Ponytail Palm/Beaucarnea recurvata	Bright Direct	Slow Grower Bulb base stores water

CHAPTER 7: HOW TO WINTERIZE A BALCONY GARDEN

So it's getting cold and you have a little balcony garden. You have some perennial plants and would like them to stay alive. Well there are some things you can do to help maintain them during the colder climates and winter months. If the plants are annuals then you throw them away. If they are perennials they will bloom again so you have to protect them.

The first consideration is to move them indoors if possible. You will need a spot in the house or apartment where you get or have ample light. Line the floor with newspaper or tinfoil before setting the pots down. If you use paper it will have to be changed because it starts to smell. If the plants have saucers already you may not need paper, the choice would be yours. Plants can be sensitive and actually bringing them indoors can shock them. You have to give them time to adjust to the different environment once you do bring them inside your home. Avoid over watering and drafts when you bring them in. The goal with winterizing perennial plants is to just keep them alive. You want to keep them in an area of your home where the temperature is relatively consistent. You can mist them regularly and keep them on a tray of gravel and water to keep the humidity regulated for them.

The perennials that are succulents and herbs should be moved indoors as soon as the temperatures start to go down. If you do not have room in your house or apartment then take some cuttings and bring them in to keep during the winter. You can replant them outside the following spring even if the plant doesn't last. This way you don't lose the whole plant. The cuttings should be kept in a lit dry area.

There are some perennials that do fine outside as long as you protect them from severe cold. The issues with plants and severe cold are:

- frost damaging leaves and tender shoots
- hard freeze killing the entire plant
- freeze/thaw action of soil disturbing the roots or cracking the container
- weight of snow or ice breaking the plant

In the case you are leaving your perennials out doors that can handle it, your aim is to try to keep them from freezing. You can't think in terms keeping them warm. A good winter temperature range for most plants is between 32F and 45F. Some vegetables do well in the chill and frost actually. Vegetables like Carrots, Lettuce, Kale, Swiss Chard, Snow Peas, Broccoli and Cabbage if planned properly can have a growing season extended into the winter months. You can't grow the seeds in winter months but if you plant the end of the summer into early fall they will extend their growth cycle to the dead of winter. Basically winter gardening means harvesting in the winter. Green houses and structures called cold frames help keep the harvests warm during the cold season. Cold frames rely on the suns energy to keep the plants alive. When all else fails you can always bring the plants inside if your space allows. A simple cold frame can be made from an old window propped up against some cinder blocks or bricks and placed around the bed of the garden.

Winterizing container perennials is also necessary if you can't bring them inside. This basically means insulating the pot by any means necessary and protecting the soil. The first thing you want to do is spread mulch over the surface soil. There are many commercial mulches to choose from. The mulch should be ground up leaves and bark and not whole leaves or large chunks. Cover the soil in your plants pots with some of the mulch. Be sure to cover it enough that the roots will be protected. If you have herbs and cannot bring them inside cover their soil very well also. Some herbs still need a lot of water, especially before the harsh winter freezes. I stated earlier it's better to bring herbs inside.

The foliage part of the plant can be covered with burlap or horticultural fleece. You can tie the fleece loosely around the pot. You can also tie loosely plastic netting around the plant and fill it around with leaves and or straw. The easiest insulator for containers would be bubble wrap or burlap. You can stuff leaves in between the pot and wrap for further insulation.

Some shrubs and perennials actually need the cold to send them into a dormant state so they can bloom or fruit the following season. So if you cannot bring your plants in there are things like I stated that can help keep them alive during the winter months.

CHAPTER 8: FERTILIZING TIPS

It is a fact that indoor plants receive a lot less light than those that grow outdoors. Because there is less light the plant is not making or using its own food sources like it would do outdoors. You have to use care when giving a plant food because the plant may not use it. Adding too much food can actually cause more harm than help. In many cases all it takes is fertilizing a plant once or twice a season to keep a plant going. In general adding a light concentration of a water soluble multipurpose fertilizer into a watering system is adequate for indoor plants unless the instructions on the plant say otherwise.

Types of Fertilizers

There are different types of fertilizers you can use with indoor plants. Here are some general categories of fertilizers that you can use based on the type of plant you have.

Tropical Plant Fertilizers for tropical plants that are indoors are concentrated with both macro and micro nutrients that are necessary for the plants.

Complete Fertilizers are fertilizers that have equal parts of three main macronutrients. They range from 8/8/8 to 20/20/20 in strength.

Chelated Fertilizers are fertilizers that are chemically bound to an agent which makes them non-ionized and water soluble. This makes the nutrients ready available to the plant.

Time Released Fertilizers are fertilizers that release nutrients over a period of time usually several months. Many potting mixtures have them.

A low dye, slow released balanced fertilizer is recommended for most plants indoors. You can use a controlled released granular fertilizer for atriums. There are also special fertilizers that are used for special conditions and plants. You have to follow the guidelines recommended by those fertilizer instructions for the best results.

Here are some general rules of thumb to follow with fertilizers:

- Do not fertilize plants less than one year after the plant was purchased from a nursery. This is because the growing media will likely contain fertilizer residues.
- Fertilize plants in moist media so the roots do not burn. It is not sufficient to water a few minutes before fertilizing. Plants should already be watered before using a fertilizer.
- Use only the recommended amounts of fertilizer.
- Palms should be fertilized in winter when new growth tips appear.
- Never fertilize diseased, stressed, or failing plants. Under these conditions we recognize that this will not reverse the situation and will probably make it worse for the plant.
- In some situations, some forms of nutrient deficiency symptoms may mimic plant illness or disease symptoms.

As plants get older the medium which is usually soil becomes compacted. Depending on the type and composition of the soil it can become water logged and unable to drain properly. It can also become rock hard and unable to absorb water. Adding new soil or medium to a plant with this kind of growing base can give it a new life. When you add new growing medium to a plant in this state you are allowing proper irrigation and air to circulate throughout the root system. It may be more effective in a case like this to fore go fertilizing the plant in this condition. In a situation like this the plant benefits more by giving it so it can once again have the capacity to receive nutrients it needs. It is also recommended that for root bound plants that dry out; to add new media to the plant. This helps the plant retain moisture too.

Potted mixtures for indoor plants are sterilized. They do not contain insects, eggs, diseases, fungi, spores or other pests. These potting mixtures are light enough to allow good draining and nutrient absorption while being heavy enough to retain nutrients and moisture. We usually think of soil when we think of the medium that supports a plants rooting system. Soil is a growing medium. A good growing medium needs to be porous, which actually means having little spaces in between the soil particles. Ideally the soil should have half of the pores filled with water and the other half filled with air and oxygen.

The next important consideration with soil is its pH balance. The acidity or alkalinity of the soil or growing medium determines how well the plant absorbs minerals from it. The pH scale ranges from 0 to 14 with 7 being neutral. 0 to 6 is acidic and 8 to 14 is alkaline. Generally tropical plants prefer a slightly acidic growing medium with a pH of 5.5 to 6.5. For all plants in general high alkalinity will cause a plant to loose leaf color and cause the growth to be stunted. On the other hand, high acidity causes wilting and abscission. You can test both the water and soil with pH testing mediums such as litmus paper. Depending on the results you can adjust to the proper pH level for the plant.

Indoor plants are also sensitive to the environmental changes like seasons outside. They are sensitive to day lengths, changes in temperature, humidity and the angle of the sun in the sky. When a plant displays new growth that's when it should be fertilized. Depending on the type of plant, the level of light, and water frequency all contributes to determining how much and how often to fertilize the plant. In the northern hemisphere particularly for tropical indoor plants the growing season is between April and December. **Do not** fertilize a plant when it is dormant like in the winter. This can damage or destroy an indoor plant.

Plants can have nutrient deficiencies like animals and humans. Deficiencies can be prevented by keeping a good fertilizing schedule.

Here is a list of some signs plants display for specific nutritional deficiencies.

Boron Deficiency: A disorder characterized by brittle, pale new leaves. Raised areas on the undersides of veins and along the petioles turn black and ooze a gummy substance. Plant usually exhibits stunted vertical growth and increased width as its terminal buds die.

Calcium Deficiency: A deficiency disease which affects the growing tips, crinkles the leaf margins and stunts the roots. Leaves may turn brown and fall off

Copper Deficiency: A deficiency disorder affecting new growth. New leaves become chlorotic with brownish margins and wilt.

Iron Deficiency: A deficiency of iron causes interveinal chlorosis (a condition where the plants leaves are pale, yellow, bleached or white looking) primarily in the newer growth. In advanced stages, the leaves may turn completely yellow or white. This sometimes happens when iron is present, but the media is too alkaline, which makes the iron unavailable to the roots.

Magnesium Deficiency: A deficiency is characterized by chlorosis, necrosis (dead tissue), stunted growth, and in some plants, a puckering and whitening of the leaves. The older leaves are affected first and turn yellow at the margins.

Manganese Deficiency: A deficiency is characterized by dwarfism, mottling, and inter veinal chlorosis of newer leaves, usually in a checked or striped pattern.

Nitrogen Deficiency: Excessive nitrogen produces soft tissues with high water content that are prone to cold damage and induces potassium deficiency. Deficiency symptoms include stunted growth, and chlorosis or yellowing, later browning of the older leaves.

Phosphorus Deficiency: A deficiency is characterized by poor root growth, and a brownish-purple coloring of the older leaves.

Potassium Deficiency: A deficiency is characterized by poor root growth and red or purple coloring of the foliage.

Zinc: A deficiency is a rare foliage disease characterized by mottling of the leaves, dwarfed and chlorotic new growth.

Chapter 9: Pruning Basics

Pruning a plant is very important in keeping it healthy and looking good. Pruning is done for size, shape, for removing diseased or dead plant material, crossing or rubbing branches and things of that nature. Remember to fertilize your plant one week before you prune it. This will encourage good growth at the location where the plant is pruned at. Your pruning equipment should always be clean and sharp. You want to make the cut two leaf nodes above soil level. A node is the small swelling that is part of the stem where the leaf emerges.

When you trim your plant try to remember what it first looked like. You want to trim a plant to its original shape. Pruning encourages new growth. If a plant grows in thickness also you may want to thin it out in the center of the plant a little. Check for broken stems. They sap the plant from nutrients and energy. If there are any remove them when pruning. You also want to cut and remove any branches or stems that grow crossing the center of the plant. Air needs to circulate throughout the plant to prevent fungal diseases. Cut the center crossed branches that interconnect with the main stem to prevent bushy growth and stubs on the branches.

When pruning a plant your clippers should run below the leaf. This will make the plant grow from the center of the stem or from the top as opposed to having long and straggly growths along the sides and irregular places. Don't be afraid to use your scissors or pruning device to remove brown leaves as well that you can't pull off easily. The plant does not feel when you cut them or need them at all. You can keep your clippers clean by dipping them in a 10 % bleach solution between each cut. This prevents disease.

Pruning should only be done when a plant is in an active growth stage except for just removing brown or dead leaves. Generally plants are not in an active growth stage during winter months. There are however winter plants and that are different. You can lightly prune (aka removing dead leaves, etc.) your plants during non-active growth months. Heavy pruning can be done in the spring and fall.

When bringing plants indoors pruning can be done to the plants advantage in September when the plants are dug up from their outdoor stations in preparation to spending the winter indoors.

Here are some guidelines on how to prune some of the more popular house plants:

Abutilon hybridum (Flowering Maple) and **Hibiscus rosa-sinensis** (China Rose) - can be pruned by cutting back the shoots of the current season about one half, or they can be pruned to its advantage after repotting them in late winter (see Fuchsia).

Chrysanthemum hortorum (Garden Chrysanthemum) - Pinch out the tips of shoots whenever they attain a length of 6 inches, until mid-July. When 1, 2, or 3 stem plants are desired, they are dis branched (removed from the main branch) as soon as the required number of main shoots has been produced by removing all side shoots when they are large enough to handle. Larger flowers are produced by dis budding, removing all but the strongest buds from each shoot.

Citrus Limonia (Ponderosa Lemon), **C. paradisi** (Grapefruit), **C. sinensis** (Sweet Orange), **C. taitensis** (Otaheite Orange) - The only Citruses commonly offered by dealers in house plants are

Ponderosa Lemon and Otaheite Orange. The Grapefruit and Sweet Orange usually are started from seeds for house plants. Pruning consists of the removal of weak, twiggy growths.

Coleus (Painted Nettle) - can be grown either as a single-stemmed plant or a branching one. Your own preference will decide which. If you are going for the for the first-named method, it will require taking out axillary shoots, as in the case of Saintpaulia; otherwise just let nature take its course, with occasional help from you in the matter of pinching out shoot tips to prevent blossoming whenever necessary. The flowers of Coleus are not attractive except for a few species such as C. thyrsoideus.

Euphorbia pulcherrima (Poinsettia) - The old plants should be cut back to within about 6 inches of the pot in April or May, repotted, and put outdoors for the summer. Cuttings may be taken from the cut-back plants during July and early August. This last method is preferable because it results in plants of moderate size. No further pruning is necessary.

Fuchsia - Resting plants should be brought into light and warmth about the end of January. When the buds start growing, repot the plants and cut back to the strongest shoots. If a bushy plant is required, the tips of the new shoots should be pinched out when they have made six or eight pairs of leaves.

Gardenia - If the plant is getting too large, prune it back one third before you set it outdoors in the spring. When the new shoots are about 6 inches long, pinch off the tips to promote branching. Do not pinch them after July.

Hedera helix - Although English Ivy, Hedera helix, can be used as a house plant, it is better to choose one of the "self-branching" mutations, such as Pittsburgh, Hahn's Self-branching, Manda's Crested, Pittsburgh Variegated, or Shamrock.

Pruning can be done by pinching out the tips of the shoots to make the plants more compact. There is a non-climbing variety, H. h. erecta, which tends toward a sprawling habit. It may require removal of some of the sprawly parts if you wish a compact plant. Rarely, it may be possible to obtain small plants of the arborescent form of English Ivy. The pruning of this requires the removal of the flowering panicles and any shoots which have reverted to the juvenile climbing habit.

Nephthytis Scindapsus aureus (Ivy Arum), **S. pictus argyraeus, Philodendron cordatum** (Heart-leaf Philodendron) - and similar climbing **Aroids** should be pruned by pinching out the tips of the shoots as soon as they are about 8 inches long. If you have large plants growing on a support, such as a tree-fern trunk, a slab with bark on it, or a stout stick with moss wired on it, wait until they reach the top of the support.

When other trailing plants such as **Cissus antarctica (**Kangaroo Vine**), C. rhombifolia** (Grape Ivy), **Ipomoea batatas (Sweet Potato), and Boussingaultia baselloides** (Madeira Vine) have reached the limits of their supports, the tips of the shoots should be pinched out to stimulate the growth of buds which otherwise would stay dormant.

Pelargonium domesticum (Lady Washington Geranium) - Shorten strong shoots in August or September and remove all weak ones. P. hortorum (House, Fish, or Zonal Geranium), when dug up in the fall, should have the top growth cut back at least one half. If they show any tendency to make lanky shoots, pinch off the tips and give them more light.

Rhododendron indicum (Greenhouse Azalea) - may be pruned immediately after flowering, but do not cut them back any more than is absolutely necessary to make a shapely bush. During the summer pinch out the tips of shoots which are outstripping their neighbors.

Saintpaulia ionantha (African Violet) - The chief pruning to be done on African Violets is that which is necessary to maintain a single-crown plant. It is best accomplished by removing the side shoots when they are barely visible, pushing them out with the aid of a pointed stick or pencil. Other pruning that may be considered desirable is the occasional removal of a wayward leaf.

Tibouchina semidecandra (Princess Tree, Glory Bush, or Spider Flower) - A plant of many aliases, which has been called by botanists **Pleroma tibouchina, P. macranthum, P. splendens, and also Lasiandra semidecandra,** has the good trait of blooming while it is still young. This can be pruned by cutting off the terminal shoots when the flowers have faded.

Hoya carnosa (Wax Plant) - needs but little pruning. Merely pinch out the tips of young shoots which are exceeding their bounds. Do not cut off the spurs (stubby growths) from which the flowers are produced.

Standard Trees

Standard trees can be trees or shrubs that have been trained to have a single trunk or they can be plants that are grafted onto a rootstock so they look like trees. Usually, the trunk is at least 3 feet tall.

- Keep the canopy in a free-flowing form.
- Prune to maintain lower older growth.
- Prune for an attractive shape.
- Prune to balance the tree. Standard trees will tip over if they are permitted to grow heavier on one side, which happens when one is placed near a window and not turned regularly, or when they are permitted to grow wide and begin to splay outward.
- Prune to keep limbs upright and straight, especially with *Ficus lyrata*.
- Prune to keep limbs from entering traffic paths or hanging over furniture which can limit the use.

Braided and Corkscrew Trunk Trees and Topiaries

- Maintain the ball or topiary shape of the plant regularly
- Consistent pruning is required to maintain the shape, weekly, if necessary.

Palms

- Cut the palm limb near the base of the stem on those that sprout from the base.
- Use pruners of an appropriate size for the plant.

- Some palms can be quite large and hard to cut with small pruners or scissors. You may need loppers or a hand saw.

Bushes

- Keep these in a natural but neat and compact form.
- Prune to maintain older lower growth and to reduce leggy appearance.
- Open "holes" in the top of the plant to allow light to reach the inside and lower areas of the plant.

Vining Plants

- Table- or cabinet-top containers and topsiders should be kept to between the rim of the container and the top of the table or cabinet.
- Base plantings around trees should be kept to within the top half of the container.
- To reduce the size of an overgrown vining plant, prune up to 1/3 of the plant back to 2 node levels above the soil line. This encourages new growth at the soil level and maintains the full look of the plant.
- To maintain the appearance and health of the plant, prune just under a leaf node at the required length.

Chapter 10: Watering Basics for Indoor Plants

Water is a very crucial resource in keeping plants alive and well. The pressure of water alone in the soil is what keeps plants standing erect. Water transports the nutrients to the plants roots, travels through the plant and then ends on the leaves and flowers.

During the transportation process of water for which plant utilizes; most of the water is absorbed by the plant roots and later evaporated off the leaves after it circulates throughout the plant. The process of water transportation for plants serve as a source of humidity and cooling of the air. Due to the fact that most indoor home environments are dry, plants indoors loose water through the transportation process via evaporation through their pores quite rapidly.

The major reason a lot of plants die and don't thrive is due to improper watering of the plant. Most of the time the wrong amount of water with the wrong watering technique for the plant leads to its demise.

Here are some general rules to follow about watering:

- When you water the plant cover the complete surface not one spot at a time
- If the plant is totally dried out, take more time to water it
- If you find that a plant in a small pot is always dry you can use "sippers" and growing media to help in this regard.
- Sippers are devices that act as stilts that are placed in the drainage holes at the bottom of a plant container. It lifts the pot and creates a

Don'ts for watering include:

- Don't dump water in one spot
- Never use very hot or very cold water
- Make sure you don't forget the edges of the plant pot
- Don't sit plants in saucers of water for more than 30 minutes After the root ball absorbs enough water discard the rest to leave it sitting in water can cause root rot

Watering a plant incorrectly can create damage on the plant, your furniture, walls and floors. Spilt water can also mean slips and falls to you as well. When plants aren't watered properly you have dead plants, rotted plants and even fungus gnats.

For those who have difficulty watering plants there are sub-irrigation systems that help water your plants. They do not have to be complicated things for example things like sippers can work just fine. It is the plant themselves that determine their watering needs.

Watering plants is an art and it takes trial and error to get it right. When you don't learn the needs of your plant it can fall victim to water stress syndrome, which is over watering one week and not enough the next. Water pressure within the plant's tissue is called "turgor" which is the plants own ability to stand erect. As the plant utilizes its water its leaves and stems stand less erect. When leaves feel cool and firm to the touch your plant has enough water. If the leaves feel soft and warm and the soil is dry then it is time to water the plant again. A plant that needs water looks droopy and like it's wilting.

The environment indoors dictates the frequency of watering. For example a low light plant living in a medium or high light environment may require more watering. Watering requirements for plants change throughout the year based on the hours of sunlight that is available naturally whether they sit in the sun or not. A plant may require weekly watering in the summer and then just once a month in the winter.

When maintaining your plants indoors, there are times when top watering the soil isn't as effective as it should be. Water sometimes does not circulate properly throughout the soil and salts builds up around the roots. Salts damage roots. The soil may be moist but there can still be a build-up of salts and fertilizers. On the other hand there are times when the water can shoot right through the soil and go into the saucer and sit there where it rots the roots. You have to stay on top of these kinds of issues to ensure a healthy plant. You have to have good drainage to help maintain healthy soil conditions. Make sure you have a pot or container that has a good sized drain hole or holes on the bottom. Most plants should not sit in water too long it is not good for them. If they do need moisture you always put something like marbles or another medium between the bottom of the pot and the saucer filled with water so the roots don't drown in the water. There are plants as I mentioned earlier in this book like the African Violet that has to be watered from the bottom up from a saucer as it sits in it for a short time directly in the water. You cannot pour water on its crown or leaves. That will kill it.

There are certain signs that show when a plant isn't receiving ample water. When the growing medium becomes too dry the plant loses the ability to absorb water properly. This results in the plant cells loose turgor resulting in wilting and droopy plants. When a plant is deprived of water longer than it should be the leaves stop functioning and then turn yellow to brown and then die. This is the natural order of leaves to give way for the younger leaves to survive. So to avoid the plant dying prematurely you have to make sure your plant does not dry out completely.

Signs of an under-watered plant are:

- Limp, warm foliage
- Brown crisp tips
- Yellowing/browning of lower foliage
- Loss of the plant's lowest older foliage
- Soil pulling away from the sides of the pot.

If your plant is displaying signs of being under-watered you can:

- Water plant until water runs into the saucer.
- Allow plant to stand in water until root ball is moistened. Add more water to the saucer as needed.
- After 30 minutes, discard remaining water.
- Note: If after 30 minutes the root ball is still dry, the roots may be compacted or root bound.
- Mist foliage with plain water to hydrate leaves.
- If a small plant uses a lot of water, such as Croton or Antherium, use deep saucers. Fill the saucer to just below the bottom of the grow pot.
- If the plant is large and requires a lot of water try a sub irrigation system

On the other hand there are also signs to let you know when a plant is being watered to death. A plant has to have oxygen at the roots to survive, just as we need oxygen to breathe. Overwatering prevents this from happening. If a plant is always wet the roots become harmed. Poisonous gases (Carbon monoxide, ethylene etc.) builds up which the roots give off as they die. The roots no longer are able to absorb water and the plant also wilts like in a drought situation as well as the leaves yellow. The difference is a dry plant comes back to life when watered, while an over watered plant suffers and decays from rotting. Most overwatering problems seem to show after 27 days after the soil is flooded with water.

The general symptoms associated with overwatering are:

- Damaged new growth
- Yellow, drooping foliage
- Black leaf tips

If the overwatering is chronic the symptoms the plant shows are:

- Soft, mushy stems or canes
- Necrotic, wet looking spots
- Excessive yellowing and black tips
- Sour smelling soil

If a plant is overwatered you can try these things:

- If saucer is full of water, dump out water.
- If decorative container has water, dump out water.
- Let plant drain until all excess water is out of the grow pot. Discard this water.
- Squeeze out excess water by gently pressing down on the growing medium.
- Wipe to clean the saucer and inside the deco pot.
- If plant smells bad (which indicates root rot), discard plant.
- Allow root ball to dry somewhat before watering again.
- If possible, increase light to the plant.

Here are some guidelines to ensure that your plants are watered properly. Plants that are in high light areas need more water, especially in direct sunlight. The same goes if the plant is in air that is hot and dry. Plants sitting on warm windowsills can actually burn, and air conditioner drafts give them cold damage. Plants in rooms with air conditioners should not be placed near the vents but do require ample water because the air is dry.

If you have plants in a tank set up, allow the tank to dry out, letting the soil dry to the point where the plant not the tank system would require watering. Fill the tank and lightly water the surface growing medium to prevent the medium from pulling away from the sides of the tank.

There are certain high moisture plants that should not be allowed to dry out. These varieties include: H*apis* Palms, Birds of Paradise, Golden or Black Bamboo, and *Podocarpus*.

Now a word on Cacti and Succulents. Succulent plants are those that store water in their leaves and stems. Cacti is the name of a large family group of plants. All Cacti are Succulents but not all Succulents are Cacti.

Succulents that are grown in containers require more water than those that are ground grown. Like all plants their watering requirements vary. In cool and cloudy weather there is less evaporation occurring in the pot and on the plant. If this type of plant is in a clay pot it will require more watering than those in plastic containers. While heat and low humidity will not damage a Succulent they go through dormant periods like all plants. This occurs when the temperature drops. Dormant Cacti need to be watered every few weeks so they don't shrivel and die.

Cacti need water especially in the spring and summer. You water them infrequently but when you do water them well. Use a soil probe to determine the moisture level of the growing media in the Cactus. If it is dry wet thoroughly and allow to dry.

Here are some watering guidelines for common Succulents:

- Ponytail palms are not palms at all. They are succulents in the Agave family. They will develop fungal root rot when kept too wet. They prefer to dry out between waterings and they tolerate dry conditions rather well.

- Jade plants can suffer root suffocation when kept too wet. The leaves begin to shrivel and the plant may become reddish in appearance with soft stems. Try to let the plant dry out fairly well between waterings.

- *Euphorbia* can thrive with little water and lots of light. Water sparingly because they can develop edema when exposed to wide fluctuations in moisture levels.

- *Sanserveria*, or snake plants, are very common house plants. They should be allowed to dry out fairly well between waterings. However, a quick way to kill a snake plant is to allow it to become completely droughted, and then water it well.

As you become familiar with your plants you will learn how to water them and know when they are dry. You will see that at some times they will require more water than others. You will also notice that when there are changes in the atmosphere there may be changes in the amounts of water required for the plant.

Chapter 11: Indoor Plants Need Light

Like plants need water they also need light. Even plants that tolerate low light still need that little bit of illumination during the course of a day so they can stay healthy. Light can come from different sources. It can come from natural sources like the sunlight that comes through the windows. It can come from overhead lighting or from artificial desk light. Natural light is brighter than artificial.

When considering where to put your plants in your home, note the direction of the window and the direction the light hits it from. It's good for a low light plant to be placed in a place that does not get direct sun. For example putting a low light in a window that faces south or west will roast that plant. Likewise putting a plant that requires a lot of light in a north facing window will make it weak because of the inadequate amount of light it receives in that direction. In places like offices and atriums light is found in the form of incandescent, fluorescent and high pressure sodium, metal halide and halogen bulbs.

For plants, the red and blue parts of the light spectrum are the most important energy sources. Plants require more from the red/orange rays of the lighting spectrum than the blue rays. Leaves of plants reflect and take a little energy from many of the yellow and green rays visible in the light spectrum as well.

So how does one determine light levels for plants anyway? Well, if you have plants near or on a windowsill; during prime times when high-levels of sun is coming in that window place a piece of white paper near the plant. If you can't put next to the plant then a table or close to the plant will be fine. Hold your hand approximately 12 inches above the paper. If your hand gets a good defined shadow that area receives bright light. If you get a muted but still clearly defined shadow you get medium light. If the shadow is barely visible you get low light in that area.

Light is measured by its intensity. The candle foot measurement is the traditional measurement of light because we used to use candle light (ft-c) foot-candles. In the lighting industry foot-candles are the common unit of measurement which is used to calculate light levels in workspaces in buildings or outdoor spaces. Instruments like light meters are used to actually measure the light intensity in foot candles. It does so by measuring the visible light that falls on the instrument.

Light bulbs list the output of lights in terms of units called lumen and lux. The information is usually on the package.

Foot Candle (ft-c)	The amount of light received by 1 square foot away from the light source
1 ft-c =	1 lumen per square foot
1 ft-c =	10.76 Lux
lux	The metric unit of the luminance of a surface
1 lux =	1 Lumen per square meter
1 lux=	0.0929 ft-c
1 lux =	0.00146 Watts per square meter

High light is defined as 300 to 400 foot candles of light. Plants that thrive in this type of light require 8 or more hours of bright light. Cacti and Succulents are high light plants. So are Croton, Yucca and Jade plants. To avoid damage of plants in high light avoid putting the plant on window sill or directly in the window. Even a couple of feet can make a difference in the intensity of the light directly on the plant. This is for plants that don't do well in intense sun light.

Medium light is defined as 200 to 300 foot candles. Plants that need medium light require six hours of light a day. *Ficus, Dracaena, Spathiphyllum*, palms, and Pothos are plants that thrive in medium light. Medium light plants do very well if given the right amount of TLC.

Low Light is defined as 75 to 200 foot candles. Low light plants require 4 hours of light a day. The light intensity for these types of plants is at reading level. Low light species include *Sanserveria*, Aspidistra, some ivies, *Spathiphyllum* and ferns.

All plants have some sort of light requirement. A plant cannot survive without light. When a plant is put in conditions that do not meet its lighting requirements it fails to thrive and eventually dies.

During the seasons the position of the sun changes. In the summer it is directly overhead; in the winter the sun is lower in the sky. It's not unusual for a plant to be situated in medium or low light in the summer and in the winter placed directly in the sunlight. This is because the sun changes its angle so the plant can be moved to meet it. Also because of natural instincts plants even if they are not in the sun directly still can tell when the seasons and angle of the sun changes.

Artificial light

When you do not have any natural sunlight in your home or good natural lighting then you have to rely on artificial means of light.

Here is a list of different types of artificial light.

Florescent
Florescent tubes provide good low to medium light for plants that require that type of light. In locations where no natural light is available it is recommended to use a combination of warm white light florescent tubes for their red spectrum rays and cool white for their blue spectrum rays. The cool whites give of very little heat so plants can stay cool. This is so even when they are placed close to the cool white.

Incandescent
Incandescent light bulbs can be used in combination with natural or other light forms. These types of light bulbs should not be the sole source of light for plants. For a plant to grow the watts should be at least 100 for an incandescent light bulb. This type of bulb gives off a lot of heat and the plant should be at least 2 feet away from this light source.

Metal Halide
Metal Halide bulbs produce a lot of light in the blue spectrum. Depending on how bright they are they support all common plants indoors.

Halogen
Halogen are light bulbs that produce light similar to the sun. This makes them an ideal plant lights. They produce a great deal of heat and the plant should not be placed too close to them. Depending on how bright they are; they can be used for all types of indoor plants.

High Pressure Sodium
These types of lights are used in commercial greenhouses as a supplemental light source to promote blooms. They produce red/orange light spectrum rays but no blue. These lights are **not** recommended for buildings indoors.

Just like watering, the lighting has to be right for a plant to thrive. If a plant is placed too far from a lighting source it will not get adequate light. The same is true if it doesn't get the right amount of hours needed in the light.

Some common signs of inadequate lighting are:

- Leggy, spindly, weak plant that may suddenly drop its leaves.
- Slowed growth.
- The lower leaves turn a lighter green, and the plant does not flower.
- Plants tend to lean towards the light source.

Plants get sunburned like people too. Here are some common signs of too much light:

- Dry patches on leaves.
- If the site gets hot enough, buds and flowers may drop off and the entire plant may wilt.

So to sum things up the amount of light a plant receives is very important. Depending on the type of plant will determine the amount of light it needs to thrive.

CHAPTER 12: CONCLUSION

Plants need care to grow and thrive indoors just as they would need outdoors. You have to take into consideration your indoor environmental factors to decide which plants fit your conditions. If you don't get much light for instance you want to pick a low light species of plant to suit your needs.

If you get seasonal light in your home then you have more plants to choose from. You can supplement the natural light in your apartment with artificial light to help maintain your plants. Also if you have a balcony, you can put your plants out in the summer and bring them in when it gets cold.

Today there are so many options available for people who love plants that there is a type of plant for all types of living situations. If you are a busy person you want a plant that doesn't require much care. But, there a plant for you as there is everyone. The main thing is to check with the plant store where you purchase your plants to make sure that the plant you are getting fits your needs and your indoor environment. Once those requirements are met you can enjoy your plant or plants in your home all year long. Hopefully with the right preparation and TLC your plants will last for years to come.

MEET THE AUTHOR

Gardener and Landscaper James Gipson has spent his last couple decades bringing beauty into the world, whether it's in his own back yard, the neighborhood playground, or over many acres surrounding a corporate office building.

In his twenties, James started a small lawn and landscaping company to make money while he was writing the great American novel. He did write his book, but what started as a necessary evil evolved into a viable—and joyful—business. Turns out James has a way with plants and soil, and soon his little company was in high demand. It wasn't long before he was hiring help and showing 5-year plans to investors. During his years in landscaping, he brought his green thumb to just about every type of garden project, but his very favorites were local parks. For James, true fulfillment was found in expressing his art while benefiting the community.

Three years ago, James gave his back a break and retired, but he still keeps up with the garden and greenhouse on his own property. Because neighborhood is important to him, he sits on his homeowner's board and is known as the "Flower Man" to the kiddos on his street. He also consults with the local park district and village boards as they beautify the parks, streets, and municipal buildings.

James lives in Tulsa, Oklahoma, with his wife of 43 years. They are blessed with a hoard of grandchildren, and fill their gardens with Easter Eggs every April. He believes families are a lot like flowerbeds—if you cultivate goodness, you usually get goodness. And he is very thankful to be living the good life.

MORE BOOKS BY JAMES GIPSON

The Ultimate Guide to Organic Gardening: Organic Gardening for Beginners

Vegetable Gardening Basics: Grow Your Own Vegetables and Save Money

www.ingramcontent.com/pod-product-compliance
Ingram Content Group UK Ltd.
Pitfield, Milton Keynes, MK11 3LW, UK
UKHW022120230426
12048UKWH00010BA/623